Friendship

By Walter E. Isenhour

Friendship is a mighty ship
That weathers many gales,
And leaves a blessing to the world
In every place it sails.
It helps the dreary, cheers the sad,
And drives dark clouds away;
It gives a helping hand to those
Who've fallen by the way.

Friendship is a blessed ship
That's full of peace and love,
And carries sunshine everywhere,
From God's own blessed above,
And makes the world a better place-
E'en more like heaven sweet-
And helps to smooth the pathway out
For weary pilgrim's feet.

Friendship

editor
van b. hooper

IDEALS PUBLISHING CO.
MILWAUKEE 1, WISCONSIN

Copyright 1961
printed and bound in U.S.A.

Salt Of The Earth

New friends I cherish
and treasure their worth,
But old friends to me
are the salt of the earth.
Friends are like garments
that everyone wears —
New ones are needed
for dress-up affairs;
But when we're at leisure,
we're more apt to choose
The clothes that we purchased
with last season's shoes.

Things we grow used to
are things we love best —
The ones we are certain
have weathered the test.
And isn't it true,
since we're talking of friends,
That new ones bring pleasure
when everything blends?
But when we want someone
who thinks as we do,
And who fits, as I said,
like last summer's shoe,
We turn to the friends
who have stuck through the years,
Who echo our laughter
and dry up our tears;
They know every weakness
and fault we possess,
But somehow forget them
in friendship's caress.

The story is old,
yet fragrant and sweet;
I've said it before,
but just let me repeat:
New friends I cherish
and treasure their worth,
But old friends to me
are the salt of the earth.

Author Unknown

The Art Of Friendship

The first step in the art of friendship is to be a friend; then making friends takes care of itself.

To be a friend a man should start by being a friend to himself, by being true to his highest and best and by aligning himself with the enduring values of human life that make for growth and progress.

To be a friend a man should strive to be "like the shadow of a great rock in a weary land," to be a source of refuge and strength to those who walk in darkness.

To be a friend a man should believe in the inherent goodness of men and in their potential greatness; he should treat men in a big spirit, expectant of a noble response.

To be a friend a man should strive to lift people up, not cast them down, to encourage, not discourage; to set an example that will be an inspiration to others.

To be a friend a man should be sensitively responsive to the dreams and aims of others and should show sincere appreciation for the contributions others make to the enrichment of his life.

To be a friend a man should practice the companionship of silence and the magic of words that his speech may build and not destroy, help and not hinder.

To be a friend a man should close his eyes to the faults of others and open them to his own.

To be a friend a man should not attempt to reform or reprimand, but should strive only to make others happy if he can.

To be a friend a man should be himself, he should be done with hypocrisy, artificiality and pretense; he should meet and mingle with people in quiet simplicity and humility.

To be a friend a man should be tolerant, he should have an understanding heart and forgiving nature, knowing that all men stumble now and then, and that he who never made a mistake never accomplished anything.

To be a friend a man should join hands with all people who are working for great principles, great purposes and great causes; he should put his shoulder to the wheel to help achieve common goals.

To be a friend a man should go more than halfway in his contacts with his fellow men; he should greet others first and not wait to be greeted; he should radiate a spirit of overflowing good will.

To be a friend a man should remember that we are human magnets; that like attracts like, and that what we give we get.

To be a friend a man should recognize that the art of friendship is a lifetime study, that no man knows all the answers, and that he should add each day to his knowledge of how to live the friendly way.

Wilferd A. Peterson

Reflections

If you walk as a friend
you will find a friend,
Wherever you choose to fare,
If you go with mirth
to a far strange land
You will find that mirth is there,
For the strangest part
of this queer old world
Is that like will join with like;
And who walks with love
for his fellow man,
An answering love will strike.

If you walk in honor,
then honest men
Will meet you along the way,
But if you are false
you will find men false
Wherever you chance to stray.
For good breeds good
and bad breeds bad,
We are met by the traits we show,
Love will find a friend
at the stranger's door,
Where hate will find a foe.

For each of us builds
the world he knows,
Which only himself can spoil,
And an hour of hate
or an hour of shame
Can ruin a life of toil,
And though to the utmost
ends of the earth
Your duty may bid you fare,
If you go with truth
and a friendly heart,
You will find friends waiting there.

Author Unknown

George Hinke
© I. P. Co. 1961

City of Dreams

Thelma Paris

There's a town far away
   called the "City of Dreams"
Where the thoughts
   of all mortals reside.
There are millions of flowers,
   each one a bright hope
For a future
   where peace will abide.

There's a stream by the town
   called the "River of Tears"
Where the heartaches
   are all washed away.
There is music to hear
   that will touch every heart,
'Tis the laughter
   of children at play.

There's a tree in this town
   called the "Promise of Life"
And its branches
   are reaching to God.
There's a vine by the tree
   that entwines it with love
And its roots travel deep
   in the sod.

There's a house in this town
   called the "Haven of Rest"
Where the restless and weary
   may dwell.
There are birds everywhere
   and they greet you with song,
Saying, "Rest. God is here.
   All is well."

Now this town far away
  is the castle you build
When your mind is so weary
  and dark,
And you wish for a carpet
  to take you away
To a land where you're free
  as a lark.

But this land that you wish for
  can be reached any day,
Not just when everything
  has gone wrong.
You can make it the place
  that you live in today,
You can make all your life
  one big song.

Just remember the town
  called the "City of Dreams"
Is made up of the treasures
  of life.
These you have all around you
  wherever you go—
Each success has its sorrow
  and strife;

Every moment well spent
  is a "promise of life";
Each smile and kind word given
  is "love";
If there's joy in your home,
  that's your "haven of rest,"
And the birds
  will sing sweetly above.

So just live everyday
  in your "City of Dreams"
Must you wait till
  the sunlight is dim?
Clasp hands with your brothers,
  and forgive all their sins,
Bow your head
  and give thanks unto Him.

Geo. Hinke

Beside My Fire

By Adam N. Reiter

Come sit beside my fire, old friend,
   And revel in its glow—
We'll watch the shadows on the screen,
   And dream of Long Ago . . .
We'll talk of things of bygone days,
   That seldom come to mind;—
Old times, old scenes, almost forgot,
   And leave the world behind!

And while we sit beside my fire
   And sniff the pungent oak—
We'll stoke our pipes with fragrant leaf,
   And watch the curling smoke.
We'll know a precious, fleeting hour
   Which lends a sweet release
From things that tend to sear and scar—
   And in their stead—find Peace!

We'll toss aside the faded years—
   We'll both be boys, again—
Forgetting all the serious things
   That haunt the realm of men.
We'll romp and play as boys must do,
   ('Though foolish it may be)
And roam the once-familiar paths;
   We two—just you and me!

Ah, there's the dusty, winding road;
   The old church on the hill—
The village store, the bridge, the creek—
   The farm-house and the mill—

And nestled low amidst the trees
   With sunbeams darting through,
And shadows playing hide and seek—
   The school-house that we knew!

But look! It's fading swiftly now—
   There's but an ember glow—
Our fire-side hour of dreams is done;
   Our fire is burning low:—
But then, 'tis something rare and fine,
   Of which I never tire . . .
A trip into the Long Ago,
   With a friend—beside my fire!

The House

By the Side of the Road

by Sam Walter Foss

There are hermit souls that live withdrawn,
In the peace of their self-content:
There are souls like stars, that dwell apart,
In a fellowless firmament;
There are pioneer souls that blaze their paths,
Where highways never ran—
But let me live by the side of the road
And be a friend to man.

Let me live in a house by the side of the road
Where the race of men go by—
The men who are good and the men who are bad,
As good and as bad as I.
I would not sit in the scorner's seat,
Or hurl the cynic's ban—
Let me live in the house by the side of the road
And be a friend to man.

I see from the house by the side of the road,
By the side of the highway of life,
The men who press with ardor of hope,
The men who are faint with the strife.
But I turn not away from their smiles nor their tears,
Both parts of an infinite plan—
Let me live in the house by the side of the road
And be a friend to man.

I know there are brook-gladdened meadows ahead,
And mountains of wearisome height;
That the road passes on through the long afternoon,
And stretches away to the night.
And still I rejoice when the travelers rejoice
And weep with the strangers that moan,
As I live in my house by the side of the road
And be a friend to man.

Tribute to a Dog

By Senator George Graham Vest

The best friend a man has in the world may turn against him and become his enemy. His son or daughter that he has reared with loving care may prove ungrateful. Those who are nearest and dearest to us, those whom we trust with our happiness and our good name may become traitors to their faith. The money that a man has, he may lose. It flies away from him perhaps when he needs it most. A man's reputation may be sacrificed in a moment of ill-considered action. The people who are prone to fall on their knees to do us honor when success is with us, may be the first to throw the stone of malice when failure settles its cloud upon our heads.

The one absolutely unselfish friend that man can have in this selfish world, the one that never deserts him, the one that never proves ungrateful or treacherous, is his dog. A man's dog stands by him in prosperity and in poverty, in health and in sickness. He will sleep on the cold ground where the wintry winds blow and the snow drives fiercely, if only he may be near his master's side. He will kiss the hand that has no food to offer; he will lick the wounds and sores that come in encounter with the roughness of the world. He guards the sleep of his pauper master as if he were a prince. When all other friends desert, he remains. When riches take wings, and reputation falls to pieces, he is as constant in his love as the sun in its journey through the heavens.

If fortune drives the master forth an outcast in the world, friendless and homeless, the faithful dog asks no higher privilege than that of accompanying him, to guard him against danger, to fight against his enemies. And when the last scene of all comes, and death takes his master in its embrace and his body is laid away in the cold ground, no matter if all other friends pursue their way, there by the graveside will the noble dog be found, his head between his paws, his eyes sad, but open in alert watchfulness, faithful and true even in death.

©

Friends

Edgar Daniel Kramer

When I turn from my tasks at dusk,
  Though cold winds blow, though lilacs bloom,
I find him waiting at the gate
  To walk with me across the gloom,
And, entering a little house,
  We leave the world and all its woe,
The while we eat our meat and bread
  Within the lamplight's mellow glow.

His eyes as bright as twinkling stars,
  He hearkens, as the kettle croons,
And, supper done, he wants to help
  To put away the plates and spoons,
But laughingly I shake my head
  And say he is a clumsy elf,
And so he wisely watches me
  Place each thing on its proper shelf.

I tamp tobacco in my pipe,
  I settle in my easychair,
And, as he sits across from me,
  I know that life is strangely fair,
In spite of tears and shattered dreams,
  In spite of selfishness and lies,
For I am finding peace and strength
  Within the trust that fills his eyes.

Although we never say a word,
  The shadows and the drifting smoke
Are startled, as they hear us laugh
  Or chuckle at some silent joke,
For hearts, that truly understand
  Each other, in a nod, a sigh,
A look are speaking fluently,
  Just as we do, — my dog and I.

Friendly Street –

By Mary Jean Shurtz

I followed a street that was wide, and led
Down a friendly way, where the folks, instead
Of thinking that they were always right,
Would admit that sometimes they were not . . . quit
And all the folks on this friendly street
Had a cheery smile when we chanced to meet
They would say "hello" in a friendly tone,
And you cared for them like your very own.
There was not one person along the way
Who would mar the happiness of the day.
And it was a place where just friends meet,
This pleasant and wide old friendly street.

And those who lived there were the kind who say,
"Well, what if he did do a wrong today?
Last night, when the rest of you were asleep,
I heard him talk and I heard him weep;
And he knelt and prayed till dawn was aflame
And still the right answer never came—
Or perhaps it WAS right—who are we to say
That it was an error he made today?"
There's a side to that and a side to this—
Couldn't we be the ones who might really miss?
Oh, it was a pleasure to meet and greet
The folks who lived on this friendly street.

But the street I followed was in a dream;
I've found that, often, in life's great scheme
Where it's made of the folks we know
Who over the rough paths, and even, go,
When the going's rough, and we sometimes make
The turn that will end in a sad mistake,
There's a good side there if we care to find
That side, instead of being so unkind.
But the man who KNOWS he is always right
And the world is wrong—and there's no respite
For the man who has strayed; will never meet
You, and cheer you on, down this friendly street.

Oh, I'd hate to be, when life here is through,
The man who was certain that only he knew
The right side of every trial that came,
And that those he chose were the ones to blame.
For I'm certain God will have mercy there
For the man who erred; and—I hope—to spare
For the man who stands at the Judgment Seat
To explain why HIS was FRIENDLY STREET.

Your Friendship

There is something in your friendship
  Very sweet for rainy days—
'Tis your thoughtfulness in finding
  What I like in little ways,
And of doing one by one,
  Things that others leave undone.

There is something in your friendship
  Sane and strong and glad and true,
Which makes better worth the doing
  Everything I have to do,
And your friendly word and smile
  Somehow helps make life worth while.

There is something in your friendship
  Very rare to find, my friend,
'Tis unselfishness in giving
  Without stint and without end;
So there is—at last I learn—
  Love that asks for no return.

There is something in your friendship
  That has stood through many a test,
Giving me a sense of safety,
  Of security and rest—
Friend of mine, my whole life through,
  I'll be glad that I met you.

Our sincere thanks to the unknown author

The friendly Way

By E. A. Guest

Oh, I would tread the friendly way,
The lanes where children romp and play,
The hearty road of fellowship
Where brotherhood is found;
I do not want the sterner game
Where life is but a fight for fame,
Nor would I quit the valleys fair
To stand on higher ground.

There is enough of riches here,
Enough of mirth and honest cheer
To balance all the hurt and pain
As time goes speeding by,
And as each day comes to its end,
If I am sure I have a friend
For greater wealth or greater fame
I shall not give a sigh.

A place to fill and work to do,
Of comrades here a loyal few,
The children glad that I'm their dad—
All that's my treasure store;
A happy home in which to live—
What further has this life to give?
And where's the rich man with his wealth
Who really gathers more?

I would not shirk nor idly stand
Before the tasks which come to hand,
I would not fail in duty's hour:
But once my work is done,
I would be father to my own,
A neighbor in my little zone,
A man among my fellowmen,
And friend to every one.

Geo. Hin

Through All The Years

JAMES W. FOLEY

Time is just a little fleeter;
Friendship just a little sweeter,
And the fruits of memory mellow
As the years and years go by.
Old friends seem a little dearer;
Hearts to hearts a little nearer,
When the leaves turn red and yellow
Underneath the autumn sky.

Dreams with recollection tender
Fill the heart with richer splendor,
As the light gleams soft in falling
Through some old cathedral dome.
And, to faults a little blinder,
We grow just a little kinder,
And the dream that's calling, calling,
Is of old friends and of home.

Friends we cling to may be fewer,
But the love for them is truer,
For we know life's richest treasure
To be friendship that endures.
And the old friends all grow dearer,
As we see with eyes grown clearer,
That joy's gladdest, fullest measure
Is a friendship such as yours.

So I smile a little longer,
And the pull's a little stronger
On my heartstrings as I sit and dream
Of some old friend and true.
With my eyes a little brighter,
And my heart a little lighter,
For the mellow lights of memory gleam
Along the trail to you.

And if time's a little fleeter,
Friendship's just a little sweeter,
And the story of its splendor
Always old and ever new.
How the years make old friends dearer,
Hearts to hearts a little nearer,
Till with friendship grown more tender
I am telling this to you.

Our sincere thanks to the author for permission before he passed on.

A Friend or Two

WILBUR D. NESBIT

There's all of pleasure and all of peace
In a friend or two,
And all your troubles may find release
With a friend or two;
It's in the grip of the clasping hand,
On native soil or in alien land,
But the world is made — do you understand —
Of a friend or two.

A song to sing and a crust to share
With a friend or two;
A smile to give and a grief to bear
With a friend or two;
A road to walk and a goal to win,
A fireside to find comfort in,
The gladdest hours that we know, begin
With a friend or two.

A little laughter, perhaps some tears,
With a friend or two;
The days, the weeks, the months and years
With a friend or two;
A vale to cross and a hill to climb,
A mock at age and a jeer at time —
The prose of life takes the lilt of rhyme
With a friend or two.

The brother-soul and the brother-heart
Of a friend or two,
Make us drift on from the crowd apart
With a friend or two;
For come days happy or come days sad,
We count no hours but the ones made glad
By the hale good times we have ever had
With a friend or two.

Then stir the fire, turn up the lamp
For a friend or two.
How glad the man who bears the stamp
Of a friend or two;
The fairest sight is a friendly face,
The blithest tread is a friendly pace,
And heaven will be a better place
For a friend or two.

©

© J. P. Co. 1961

When You Get "On" —

When you get "on" and you've lived a long time
And the walk up the stairs is a mighty high climb,
Though your eyes are dimmer than what they were
And the page of a book has a misty blur,
Strange as the case may seem to be,
Then is the time you will clearly see.

You'll see yourself as you really are,
When you've lived a lot and you've traveled far,
When your strength gives out and your muscles tire
You'll see the folly of ambition's desire;
You'll see what now to your sight is hid,
The numberless trivial things you did.

Often the blindest are youthful eyes,
For age must come ere a man grows wise,
And youth makes much of the mountain peaks,
And the strife for fame and the goal it seeks,
But age sits down with the setting sun
And smiles at the boastful deeds it's done.

You'll sigh for the friends that were turned aside
By a hasty word or a show of pride,
You'll laugh at medals that now you prize,
For you'll look at them through clearer eyes
And see how little they really meant
For which so much of your strength was spent.

You'll see, as always an old man sees,
That the waves die down with the fading breeze,
That the pomps of life never last for long,
And the great sink back to the common throng,
And you'll understand when the struggle ends,
That the finest gifts of this life are friends.

Author Unknown

To An Old Friend's House

Adam N. Reiter

It's never far to an old friend's house,
    And the way is smooth and fine,
The path bears many a telltale mark
    Of footprints . . . his and mine—
Each hill and vale and winding curve,
    Its youthful fancies lend,
And miles are short, when I go forth
    To the house of an old, old friend.

The day is always bright and fair,
    When I, on a friend would call,
Who's been a friend in time and stress
    And "stood by"—through it all—
'Though skies are drear and clouds hang low,
    And the outlook, drab and gray;
There's a radiant glow at an old friend's house,
    That drives the gloom away.

Time never drags at an old friend's house,
    And the hours are filled with joy,
He pictures me, and I picture him
    As a carefree, laughing boy—
Old faces beam with wrinkled smiles,
    And the long years brightly blend
In a wealth of treasured memories—
    At the house of an old, old friend!

©

That Old, Old Friend of Mine—

Frank D. Felt

There are many priceless jewels
We may covet day by day,
And many worldly treasures
That we gather by the way,
But of all this life's possessions
That human hearts defend,
There is none I hold more dearly
Than a certain old, old friend.

A friend I've always reached for
As I've stumbled o'er the trails,
And found a hand of welcome
From a heart that never fails;
For friendship that is rooted
Deep into the mellow past,
Like the rugged timeless pine tree,
Holds its virtue — to the last.

A friendship that was nourished
By the many trying years,
That has ever grown and flourished
Through the seasons smiles and tears,
With a sort of understanding,
Veiling all our human pride,
And I could open up my heart
Where troubles often hide.

Some friends just fit the contours
'Round a worn and weary heart,
Like our old and favorite ridin' boots
From which we dread to part,
And he's never changed by fortune,
Nor swayed with worldly fame,
His smile still like the sunshine,
He's always just the same.

Ah! there were times at our house
When life looked cold and grim,
But our humble hearthside seemed to glow
At just the sight of him,
There were many laughs and chuckles,
A frown — and oft' a sigh,
As we'd dig into life's treasure chest,
Those golden days gone by.

And I would that he might understand,
Ere all our days are spent,
How I've treasured his acquaintance —
Just what his smiles have meant;
For those memories I cherish,
Like the sweetest, rarest wine
That I sip in recollections,
Of that old, old friend of mine.

Leavin' the Old and Greetin' the New

Lawrence Hawthorne

It's kind o' tough t' have t' leave
So many folks you've learned t' know,
An' have 'em grip yer hand an' tell
How much they hate t' see you go!
It's kind o' tough t' say goodbye
To friends you've seen day after day—
It's hard t' break the happy bonds
O' comradeship an' move away.

It's hard t' pack up all yer things
An' leave a cozy home behind—
The place where joys have come t' you,
Where neighbors all have been so kind.
An' when, at last, yer dearest pal
Is tryin' hard t' make a bluff
At bein' brave, an' breaks right down—
It's kind o' tough, it's kind o' tough!

But say! It's great t' find new friends,
Jus' waitin' fer a chance t' show
How glad they are t' have you come
An' live with 'em! It's great t' know
That folks 're just about the same
No matter where you chance t' roam,
An' if you let 'em have their way,
You'll soon be feelin' right at home.

So, it's a long farewell, old friends;
May God be mighty good t' you!
Across the miles an' down the years
You'll find my friendship always true.
And now I turn with eager heart
T' meet whatever life extends—
T' greet the folks that welcome me,
An' try t' make them all my friends.

©

It's A Pretty Good Plan
—To Forget It!

If you see a tall fellow
ahead of the crowd,
A leader of men
marching fearless and proud,
And you know of a tale
whose mere telling aloud
Would cause this proud head
to in anguish be bowed,
It's a pretty good plan
to forget it!

If you know of a skeleton
hidden away
In a closet, and guarded
and kept from the day
In the dark, whose showing,
whose sudden display
Would cause grief and sorrow
and lifelong dismay—
It's a pretty good plan
to forget it!

If you know of a spot
in the life of a friend,
(We all have such spots
concealed, world without end),
Whose touching his heartstrings
would play on and rend
Till the shame of its showing
no grieving could mend,
It's a pretty good plan
to forget it!

If you know anything
that will darken the joy
Of a man or a woman,
a girl or a boy,
That will wipe out a smile
or the least way annoy
A fellow, or cause
any gladness to cloy,
It's a pretty good plan
to forget it!

Author Unknown

I Made A Friend Today

Douglas Malloch

If I could make a friend today
I would not ask for greater store,
If just one soul would come and say,
"We shall be comrades evermore,"
I would not need to count my gold
Tonight when busy labors end—
My heart a greater wealth would hold
If I could say, "I made a friend."

If I could have a friend tonight
I did not have at this day's dawn,
One hand that held my own as tight,
One breast that I could lean upon,
I would not need to calculate
The daily profit, worth of trade,
Tomorrow's gain to estimate,
If I could say, "A friend I made."

If I today a friend could find
Amid the labor and the stress,
Some toiling brother, kindred mind,
Some hand to clasp in tenderness,
It would not matter what reward
The hours had brought me on the way
If I could say, "I thank Thee, Lord—
I know I made a friend today."

My Purpose

Henrietta Heron

To be a little kindlier
With the passing of each day;
To leave but happy memories
As I go along my way;
To use possessions that are mine
In service full and free;
To sacrifice the trivial things
For larger good to be;
To give of love in lavish way
That friendship true may live;
To be less quick to criticize,
More ready to forgive;
To use such talents as I have
That happiness may grow;
To take the bitter with the sweet,
Assured 'tis better so;
To be quite free from self-intent
Whate'er the task I do;
To help the world's faith stronger grow,
In all that's good and true;
To keep my faith in God and right
No matter how things run;
To work and play and pray and trust
Until the journey's done.
God grant to me the strength of heart,
Of motive and of will,
To do my part and falter not
His purpose to fulfill.

Our sincere thanks to the author
whose address we were unable to locate.

Those Good Folks

Phil Perkins

When th' evening shadows lengthen
And th' nighttime settles down,
I like to sit and ponder
On th' good folks in our town—

Th' folks who have a moment
For th' children at their play,
And wave a cheery greeting
As they pass along th' way.

The kind of worthy people
Who would always be your friend,
Good folks who'd never fail you—
Who'd be faithful to th' end.

Ah, yes, I like to ponder
When th' evening stars appear,
On th' good folks of th' village
Who spread happiness and cheer.

Th' folks who never falter
When there's something they may do—
A burden to be lifted,
Or a friendship to renew.

Th' kindly folks who linger
At your bedside when you're ill,
And think of naught but comfort
As they do your bid an' will.

My heart is very happy,
As th' moon beams from above,
For th' good folks 'round about me,
For their kindness and their love.

For it truly is a blessing
To have neighbors dwelling near,
Who are always spreading sunshine
With a word and smile sincere.

And I hope when shadows deepen
And my bark puts out to sea,
I'll be guided to that harbor
Where good folks may welcome me.

From an old scrapbook.
Author's address unknown.

Three Wishes

Henry Turner Bailey

A fairy allows me three wishes,
Three wishes for a friend;
Now, honest and true, that must be you,
So three to you I send.

I wish you a body so healthy
That living is pure delight;
Your work every day like happy play;
Your sleep like a child's at night.

I wish you a mind so responsive
That nothing escapes your ken;
The Creator's plan, nor the notes of Pan,
Nor the good in your fellow men.

I wish you a heart prone to loving,
That all may be dear to you;
Your friends indeed, all those you need,
And those who need you, too.

I've wished you my three best wishes,
But the three are really one;
God grant you wealth — just perfect health,
Until your day is done.

From an old scrapbook.
Our sincere thanks to the author
whose address we could not locate.

Old Friends

David Banks Sickles

There are no friends like old friends,
And none so good and true;
We greet them when we meet them,
As roses greet the dew;
No other friends are dearer,
Though born of kindred mold;
And while we prize the new ones,
We treasure more the old.

There are no friends like old friends,
Where'er we dwell or roam,
In lands beyond the ocean,
Or near the bounds of home;
And where they smile to gladden,
Or sometimes frown to guide,
We fondly wish those old friends
Were always by our side.

There are no friends like old friends,
To calm our frequent fears,
When shadows fall and deepen
Through life's declining years;
And when our faltering footsteps
Approach the Great Divide,
We'll long to meet the old friends
Who wait on the other side.

©

The Friendly Things

Author Unknown

Oh, it's just the little homely things,
The unobtrusive, friendly things,
The "Won't-you-let-me-help-you" things
That make our pathway light.

The "Laugh-with-me-it's-funny" things
And it's the jolly, joking things,
The "Never-mind-the-trouble" things,
That make the world seem bright.

For all the countless famous things
The wondrous record-breaking things,
These "never-can-be-equaled" things
That all the papers cite.

Are not the little human things,
The "everyday encountered" things,
The "just-because-I-like-you" things,
That make us happy quite.

So here's to all the little things,
The "done-and-then-forgotten" things,
Those "oh-it's-simply-nothing" things
That make life worth the fight.

Greetings For Two

James W. Foley

Knowed him more'n twenty year',
Liked him through an' through;
Him an' me was neighbors here
When th' land was new.
He druv' past here every day,
Wave' his hand jes' so;
Then he'd holler, "Howdy!" an'
I'd holler back, "Hello!"

I'd be workin' in th' field,
He'd be off to town;
An' I'd hear the rattle-wheeled
Buggy comin' down;
I'd look up from hoein' corn,
An' I'd see him go;
Then he'd holler, "Howdy!" an'
I'd holler back, "Hello!"

Never was no other talk
Had by him an' me;
See him go by, trot er walk,
Wave — an' let him be.
Alwus knowed when I looked up
Jest how it 'u'd go:
He 'u'd holler, "Howdy!" an'
I'd holler back, "Hello!"

Say, I call that neighborin'
In th' proper way;
Ain't no kith o' mine er kin
Fur as I kin say;
Always friendly, cheery-like,
Sunshine, rain, er snow,
He jest hollers, "Howdy!" an'
I holler back, "Hello!"

He 'ten's to his own affairs,
An' I 'ten' t' mine;
He don't put on any airs,
I don't cut no shine;
Weather bad er weather fair,
Drivin' fast er slow,
He jest hollers, "Howdy!" an'
I holler back "Hello!"

That's th' way we started out
When we settled here;
Like t' keep it up about
'Nother twenty year',
Look — out yonder in the road —
There! Now see him go!
Soon he'll holler, "Howdy!" an'
I'll holler back, "Hello!"

Our sincere thanks to the author who granted permission to feature his poems before he passed on.

That's A Friend

John Burroughs
(1837-1921)

One whose grip is a little tighter,
One whose smile is a little brighter,
One whose deeds are a little whiter,
That's what I call a friend.

One who'll lend as quick as he'll borrow,
One who's the same today as tomorrow,
One who'll share your joy and sorrow,
That's what I call a friend.

One whose thoughts are a little cleaner,
One whose mind is a little keener,
One who avoids those things that are meaner,
That's what I call a friend.

One, when you're gone, who'll
    miss you sadly,
One who'll welcome you back
    again gladly,
One who, though angered, will
    not speak madly,
That's what I call a friend.

One who is always willing to aid you,
One whose advice has always paid you,
One who's defended when others flayed you,
That's what I call a friend.

One who's been fine when
    life seemed rotten,
One whose ideals you have
    not forgotten,
One who has given you more
    than he's gotten,
That's what I call a friend.

©

I only want a chosen few . . . Who've stood through good and evil, too . . . True friendship's test . . . Who only strove to find the good . . . And then as only true friends could . . . Forgave the rest.

❀

There's a time to get, and a time to give . . . And a time to throw away . . . There's a time to do a kindly deed . . . And that time is today . . . There's a time to sing and a time to mourn . . . A time for joy and sorrow . . . There's a time to love; but the time to hate . . . Might better be tomorrow . . . There's a time to sleep and a time to wake . . . A time to work and play . . . But the time to speak an evil thought . . . Passed by us yesterday.

Author Unknown

❀

If I had known what trouble you were bearing . . . What griefs were in the silence of your face . . . I would have been more gentle and more caring . . . And tried to give you gladness for a space . . . I would have brought more warmth into the place . . . If I had known.

If I had known what thoughts despairing drew you . . . Why do we never understand . . . I would have lent a little friendship to you . . . And slipped my hand within your lonely hand . . . And made your stay more pleasant in the land . . . If I had known.

Mary Carolyn Davies

Friendship is a chain of God . . . Shaped
in God's all perfect mold . . . Each link a
smile, a laugh, a tear . . . A grip of the
hand, a word of cheer . . . Steadfast as the
ages roll . . . Binding closer soul to soul . . .
No matter how far or heavy the load . . .
Sweet is the journey on friendship's road.

Author Unknown

*

*It's the giving and doing for somebody else
. . . On that, all life's splendor depends . . .
And the joys of this life, when you sum them
all up . . . Are found in the making of friends.*

Author Unknown

*

*Give me a few friends who will love me for
what I am, or am not, and keep ever burning
before my wandering steps the kindly light
of hope. And though age and infirmity over-
take me, and I come not in sight of the castle
of my dreams; teach me still to be thankful
for life and time's old memories that are
good and sweet. And may the evening twi-
light find me gentle still.*

Author Unknown

*

When good friends walk beside us . . . On the
trails that we must keep . . . Our burdens seem
less heavy . . . And the hills are not so steep
. . . The weary miles pass swiftly . . . Taken in
a joyous stride . . . And all the world seems
brighter . . . When friends walk by our side.

Author Unknown

*

Since it has been my lot to find . . . At every
parting of the road . . . The helping hand of
comrade kind . . . To help me with my heavy
load . . . And since I have no gold to give
. . . And love alone must make amends . . .
My humble prayer is, while I live . . .
"God make me worthy of my friends."

Author Unknown

*

We get the sweetest comfort . . . When we
wear the oldest shoe . . . We love the old
friends better . . . Than we'll ever love the new
. . . Old songs are more appealing . . . To the
wearied heart — and so . . . We find the sweetest music . . . In the tunes of long ago . . .
There's a kind of mellow sweetness . . . In a
good thing growing old . . . Each year that
rolls around it . . . Leaves an added touch
of gold.

Author Unknown

*

Tomorrow is not promised us . . . So let us
take today . . . And make the very most of it
. . . The once we pass this way . . . Just speak
aloud the kindly thought . . . And do the
kindly deed . . . And try to see and understand . . . Some fellow creature's need . . .
Tomorrow is not promised us . . . Nor any
other day . . . So let us make the most of it
. . . The once we pass this way.

Louise Mae Hogan
©

*

A friend is a present you give yourself.

Robert Louis Stevenson

*

*It's the kindly hearts of men that make . . .
This good old world worthwhile . . . It's the
friendly lips with words that make . . . The
care-erasing smile . . . And I ask myself this
question . . . When my goodly gift I see . . . Am
I a friend to as many men . . . As have been
good friends to me?*

*When my brothers speak a word of praise . . .
My wavering will to aid . . . I ask if ever their
long, long ways . . . My words have brighter
made . . . And to my heart I bring again . . .
This eager, earnest plea . . . Make me a friend
to as many men . . . As have been good friends
to me.*

Samuel H. Brown

❧

*It's the hand we clasp with an honest grasp
. . . That gives us a hearty thrill . . . It's
the good we pour into others' lives . . . .
That comes back our own to fill . . . It's
the dregs we drain from another's cup . . .
That makes our own seem sweet . . . And
the hours we give to another's need . . .
That make our life complete.*

*It's the burdens we help another bear . . .
That make our own seem light . . . It's the
danger seen for another's feet . . . . That
shows us the path to right . . . It's the good
we do each passing day . . . With a heart
sincere and true . . . In giving the world
your very best . . . Its best will return to you.*

Author Unknown

❧

*There's nothing like a greeting . . . From folks who
truly care . . . To keep the good old Friendship Trail
. . . In excellent repair.*

An Ancient Prayer

Give us, Lord, a bit o' sun,

A bit o' work and a bit o' fun;

Give us all in th' struggle and splutter

Our daily bread and a bit o' butter;

Give us health, our keep to make

An' a bit to spare for poor folks' sake;

Give us sense, for we're some of us duffers,

An' a heart to feel for all that suffers;

Give us, too, a bit of a song

An' a tale, and a book to help us along.

An' give us our share o' sorrow's lesson,

That we may prove how grief's a blessin'.

Give us, Lord, a chance to be

Our goodly best, brave, wise and free,

Our goodly best for ourselves and others,

Till all men learn to live as brothers.

When You Get

Edgar A. Guest

When you get to know a fellow,
    know his joys and his cares,
When you've come to understand him
    and the burdens that he bears,
When you've learned the fight he's making
    and the troubles in his way,
Then you find that he is different
    than you thought him yesterday.

You find his faults are trivial
    and there's not so much to blame
In the brother that you jeered at
    when you only knew his name.
You are quick to see the blemish
    in the distant neighbor's style,
You can point to all his errors
    and may sneer at him the while.

And your prejudices fatten
    and your hates more violent grow
As you talk about the failures
    of the man you do not know,
But when drawn a little closer,
    and your hands and shoulders touch,
You find the traits you hated
    really don't amount to much.

To Know A Fellow

When you get to know a fellow,
   know his every mood and whim,
You begin to find the texture
   of the splendid side of him;
You begin to understand him,
   and you cease to scoff and sneer,
For with understanding always
   prejudices disappear.

You begin to find his virtues
   and his faults you cease to tell,
For you seldom hate a fellow
   when you know him very well.
When next you start in sneering
   and your phrases turn to blame,
Know more, before you censure,
   of his business and his name.

For it's likely that acquaintance
   would your prejudice dispel,
And you'd really come to like him
   if you knew him very well.
When you get to know a fellow
   and you understand his ways,
Then his faults won't really matter,
   for you'll find a lot to praise.

©

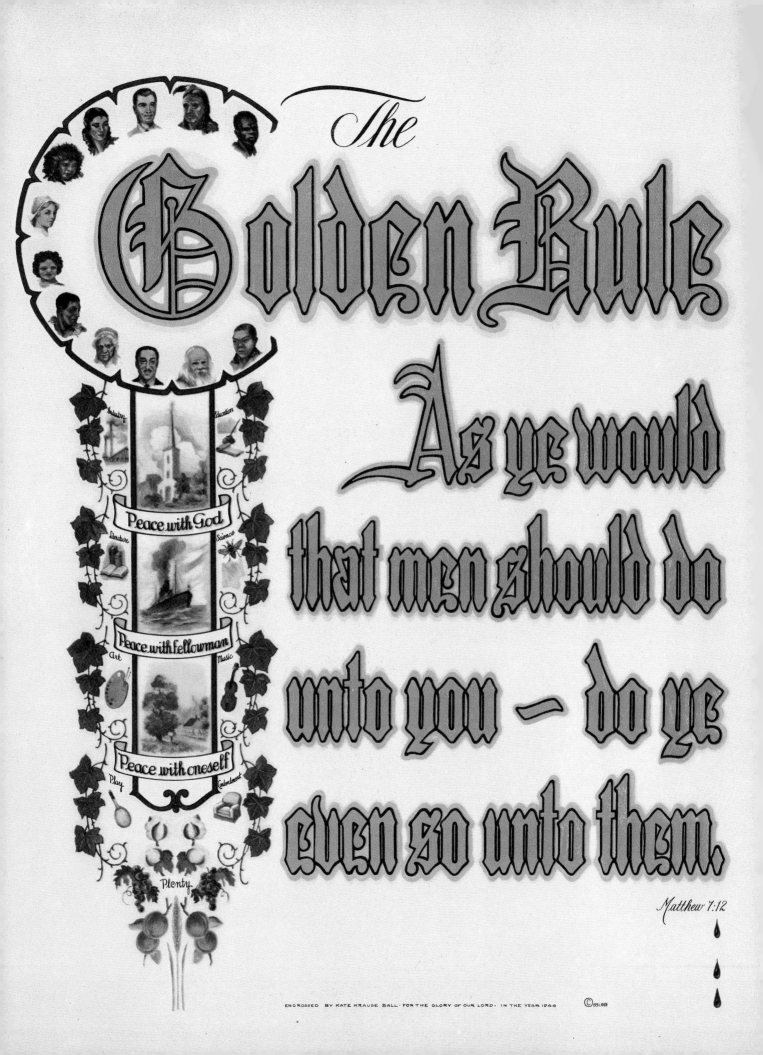

The Golden Rule

As ye would that men should do unto you — do ye even so unto them.

Peace with God

Peace with fellowman

Peace with oneself

Industry · Education · Literature · Science · Art · Music · Play · Contentment · Plenty

Matthew 7:12

These are some of my favorites— I hope you will enjoy them, too—

The road of life sometimes grows steep,
And our steps begin to slow,
As we seek amid daily toil and strife
Greater happiness to know.

We search the path on either side,
Or look toward the gleam ahead,
For an ever elusive will-o'-the-wisp,
When it lies close at hand, instead.

Genuine happiness dwells in our hearts,
We need not seek it afar,
By rendering service to others,
We will find it, right where we are.

Lola M. Hazard
©

❦

Begin the day with friendliness,
Keep friendly all day long.
Keep in your soul a friendly thought,
In your heart a friendly song.
Have in your mind a word of cheer
For all who come your way,
And they will greet you, too, in turn
And wish you a happy day.

Author Unknown

Friendship needs no studied phrases,
Polished face, or winning wiles;
Friendship deals no lavish praises,
Friendship dons no surface smiles.

Friendship follows nature's diction,
Shuns the blandishments of art,
Boldly severs truth from fiction,
Speaks the language of the heart.

Friendship favors no condition,
Scorns a narrow-minded creed,
Lovingly fulfills its mission,
Be it word or be it deed.

Friendship — pure, unselfish friendship,
All through life's allotted span,
Nurtures, strengthens, widens, lengthens,
Man's affinity with man.

Author Unknown

❦

Man strives for glory, honor, fame,
That all the world may know his name.
Amasses wealth by brain and hand;
Becomes a power in the land.

But when he nears the end of life
And looks back o'er the years of strife,
He finds that happiness depends
On none of these, but love of friends.

Author Unknown

Say It Now

If you have a friend worth loving,
Love him. Yes, and let him know
That you love him, ere life's evening
Tinge his brow with sunset glow.
Why should good words ne'er be said
Of a friend — till he is dead?

If you hear a song that thrills you,
Sung by any child of song,
Praise it. Do not let the singer
Wait deserved praises long.
Why should one who thrills your heart
Lack the joy you may impart?

If you hear a prayer that moves you
By its humble, pleading tone,
Join it. Do not let the seeker
Bow before his God alone.
Why should not your brother share
The strength of "two or three" in prayer?

If you see the hot tears falling
From a brother's weeping eyes,
Share them. And by kindly sharing
Own your kinship in the skies.
Why should anyone be glad
When a brother's heart is sad?

If a silvery laugh goes rippling
Through the sunshine on his face,
Share it. 'Tis the wise man's saying —
For both grief and joy a place.
There's health and goodness in the mirth
In which an honest laugh has birth.

If your work is made more easy
By a friendly, helping hand,
Say so. Speak out brave and truly
Ere the darkness veil the land.
Should a brother workman dear
Falter for a word of cheer?

Scatter thus your seeds of kindness
All enriching as you go —
Leave them. Trust the Harvest Giver;
He will make each seed to grow.
So, until the happy end,
Your life shall never lack a friend.

Author Unknown

❀

We cannot change yesterday,
  that is quite clear
Nor begin on tomorrow until it is here —
So all that is left for you and for me
Is to make today as sweet as can be.

Author Unknown

I would like to send you a sunbeam,
Or the twinkle of some bright star,
Or a tiny piece of the downy fleece
That clings to a cloud afar.

I would like to send you the essence
Of myriad sunkissed flowers,
Or the lilting song, as it flows along,
Of a brook through fairy bowers.

I would like to send you the dewdrops
That glisten at break of day,
And then at night the eerie light
That mantles the Milky Way.

I would like to send you the power
That nothing can o'erthrow . . .
The power to smile and laugh the while
As trav'ling thro' life you go.

But these are just wild wishes;
So I'll send you a mere Godspeed,
I'll clasp your hand, then you'll understand
All the things I have left unsaid.

Author Unknown

❀

GOOD MORNIN'

Tho' the day is dark and gloomy
And you're on a downward trend,
Put a twinkle in your eye
And say "Good Mornin'" to a friend.

When the clouds are hanging heavy
In the sky and in your heart,
Say "Good Mornin'" to somebody —
Give his day a brighter start.

Soon you'll find yourself a-smilin'
When you never thought you could,
And your friends will see the sunshine
When they never thought they would.

There is sunshine deep inside you,
If you only let it through
It will shine out like a halo,
You'll be happy if you do.

Don't let the weatherman predict you
Like the weather that he sends —
Put a twinkle in your eye
And say "Good Mornin'" to your friends!

by Wanda Mary Jaragosky

©

Life is made sweet because
of friends we have made,
And the things which
in common we share.
We want to live on,
not because of ourselves,
But because of
the people who care.
It's in giving and doing
for somebody else —
On that all life's splendor
depends,
And the joys of this life,
when you've summed it all up,
Are found in the
making of friends.

Grace Walter Clarke

❀

A friendship is a precious thing . . . too precious to destroy . . . a hasty word can spoil it all . . . and crush life's greatest joy . . . To have a friend is to be blessed, life can never be grey . . . if you've a friend to take your arm and help you on the way . . . A friend will share your failures, and will share your triumphs too . . . There is no thought of jealousy in friendship that is true . . . So if you've quarreled with your friend, take up your pen today . . . and write a little friendly note . . . you'll know just what to say . . . Don't hug your foolish pride . . . sometimes it's weakness to be strong . . . it doesn't really matter who was right or who was wrong . . . Love is the only thing that really matters in the end . . . So make this day a happy day and make up with your friend.

Patience Strong

©

❀

There's nothing cheers a fellow up
just like a hearty greeting —
A handclasp and an honest smile
that flash the joy of meeting;
And when at friendly doors you ring,
somehow it seems to free you
From all life's doubts to hear them say:
"Come in! We're glad to see you!"

Where there is room in the heart there is
always room in the house.

Sir Thomas Moore

❀

There's nothing so bad
that it could not be worse;
There's little that time
may not mend,
And troubles, no matter
how thickly they come,
Most surely will come
to an end.

You've stumbled — well,
so have we all in our time.
Don't dwell overmuch
on regret,
For you're sorry, God knows —
well, leave it at that —
Let past things be past,
and forget.

Don't despond, don't give up,
but just be yourself —
The self that is highest
and best.
Just live every day
in a sensible way,
And then leave to God
all the rest.

Author Unknown

❀

You call me friend . . .
But do you realize
How much the name implies . . .
It means that down the years,
Through sunshine and through tears,
There's always someone standing by your
*   heart.*
You call me friend . . .
And thus your life and mine
Grows richer in design . . .
And I would have you know,
Wherever you may go,
There's always someone standing by your
*   heart.*

Hilda Butler Farr

©

❀

Brows may wrinkle, hair grow gray —
But friendship never knows decay.

A TEST OF FRIENDSHIP

If a friend of mine gave a feast, and did not invite me to go to it, I should not mind a bit. But if a friend of mine had a sorrow and refused to allow me to share it, I should feel it most bitterly. If he closed the doors of the house of mourning against me, I would move back again and again and beg to be admitted, so that I might share in what I was entitled to share. If he thought me unworthy, unfit to weep with him, I would feel it as the most poignant humiliation, as the most terrible mode for which disgrace could be inflicted on me ... he who can look on the loveliness of the world and share its sorrow, and realize something of the wonder of both, is in immediate contact with divine things, and has got as near to God's secret as anyone can get.

Oscar Wilde

❦

The best way to have a friend is for you to be one.

❦

Friendship is not merely one of life's ornaments. It is one of the very essentials upon which life is founded. To have true friends is not a matter of chance. We have them solely because our character and actions are of such high standards that men are drawn toward us, just as steel filings leap toward the magnet.

The man who has no friends has made a mistake somewhere along life's journey. His life may have been such as to render him unworthy of friends or he has been too proud or self-centered to welcome friendship with his fellow men. In either case, there is bound to be a good reason for such a condition to exist in his life.

Our friends are among the choicest possessions life has bestowed upon us, and we should use the greatest possible care in preserving them. It is our duty to exert every effort to retain old friends and to make new ones. Someone has truly said that great is the fellowship along that highway of life known as friendship's road.

Author Unknown

Did you give him a lift?
He's a brother of man
And bearing all the burden he can.
Did you give him a smile?
He was downcast and blue,
And a smile would have helped him
to battle it through.
Did you give him a hand?
He was slipping down hill,
And the world, so I fancied,
was using him ill.
Did you give him a word?
Did you show him the road?
Or did you just let him
go on with his load?

S. B. Cooney
Address Unknown

❦

Give me a friend and I'll worry along,
My vision may vanish,
my dream may go wrong;
My wealth I may lose,
or my money may spend;
But I'll worry along,
if you give me a friend.

Give me a friend,
and my youth may depart
But still I'll be young
in the house of my heart,
Yes, I'll go laughing
right on to the end,
Whatever the years,
if you give me a friend.

Author Unknown

❦

Oh, it's great to have a friend
like you along life's weary road,
One who is always kind and true,
to help me bear my load.
It's great to have a friend like you
while traveling here below,
One who tries to help me through
as on my way I go.
It's great to have a friend like you
as I journey through this life;
I thank you now for all you do
to banish doubt and strife.
I'd like to have more friends like you —
true-blue until the end;
And if my wish will e'er come true —
I shall be such a friend.

Author Unknown